Frances Stark
My Best Thing

Koenig Books
Contemporary Art Gallery
The Banff Centre

Foreword

First presented in ILLUMInations at the 54th Venice Biennale, *My Best Thing* by Frances Stark has rapidly gained critical attention. The feature-length animation continues the artist's ongoing concerns with expectation and gender, infused with notions of doubt, anxiety and musings on the general state of things. While arguably best known for her works on paper, with such issues seen through the lens of writing, collage and drawing, her videos and performance pieces likewise comprise a forceful component in her overall artistic proposition.

In *My Best Thing* a conversation unfolds between two online avatars, a man and a woman, playmobil-like figures wearing discrete fig leaves for modesty. Their flirtatious chat-room dialogue quickly moves beyond sex to discuss ideas of history, politics, collaboration and the very act of art-making itself. Created from actual chats between a number of individuals, these have been transferred via text-to-speech animation software to make a compelling work that poignantly and humorously touches on our changing world; a place where relationships mediated by technology challenge the usual understanding of how we interact with each other and allow new forms of behaviour to emerge.

And so we too celebrate a coming together joined by mutual desire, albeit in this instance a shared interest in the opportunity to work with Stark. For the Walter Phillips Gallery at The Banff Centre and the Contemporary Art Gallery, Vancouver, this partnership marks a common recognition of the importance of writing and publication as a means to expand the critical reception of artists' work. The focus of this book centres on the commissioning of a major new text that elucidates a shared space for such encounters. We thank Mark Godfrey for his insightful essay where ideas of performance and role-playing, the anonymity versus intimacy implicit within Stark's video, are examined and brought into the wider philosophical discourse of subjectivity where strangers can so easily transform into confidantes.

Above all we thank Frances Stark. Her wit and the persuasive nature of her work provide an ongoing reminder to us all of the complexity of everyday encounters.

Nigel Prince
Executive Director, Contemporary Art Gallery

Kitty Scott
Director Visual Arts, Creative Residencies, Banff International Curatorial Institute, Walter Phillips Gallery, The Banff Centre

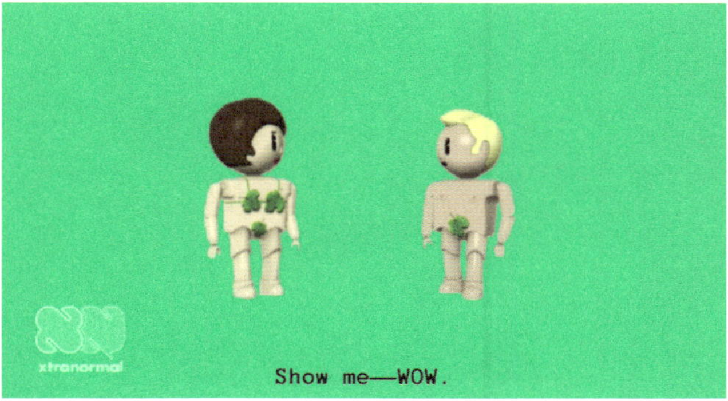
xtranormal
Show me—WOW.

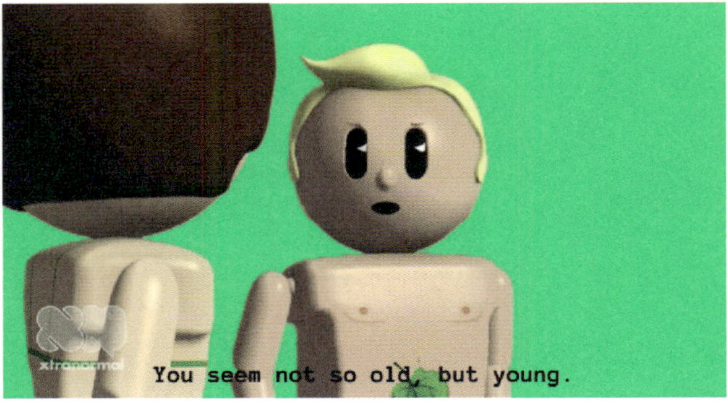
xtranormal
You seem not so old, but young.

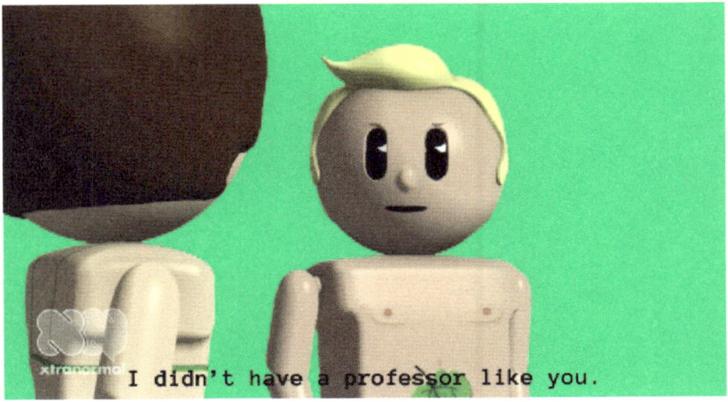
I didn't have a professor like you.

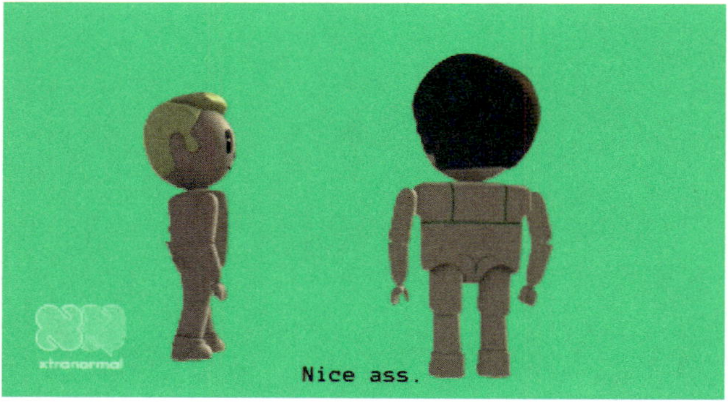
xtranormal
Nice ass.

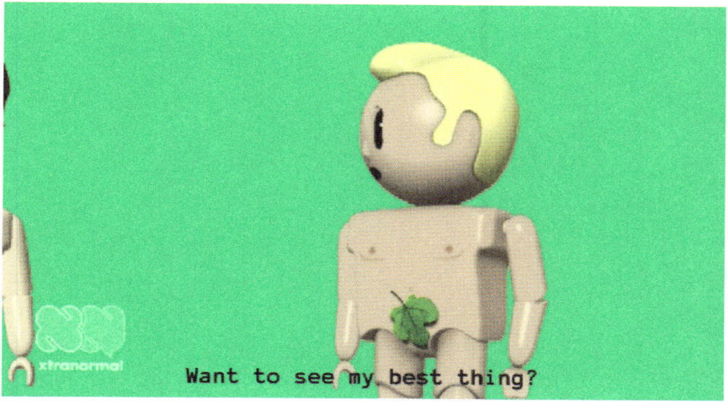
xtranormal
Want to see my best thing?

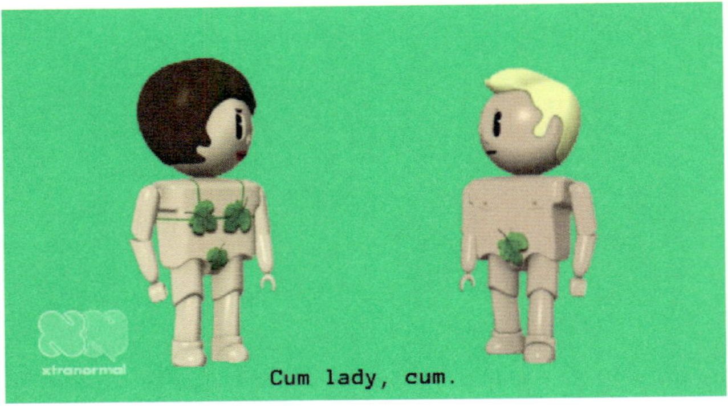
xtranormal
Cum lady, cum.

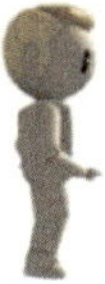

In the previous episode, a young man showed a woman his best thing. She told him she might be invited to the Venice Biennale, he thought she meant the film one, but she meant the art one. He joked he would one day win a prize in the film one.

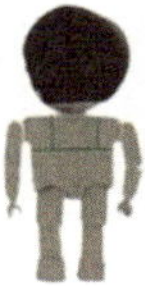

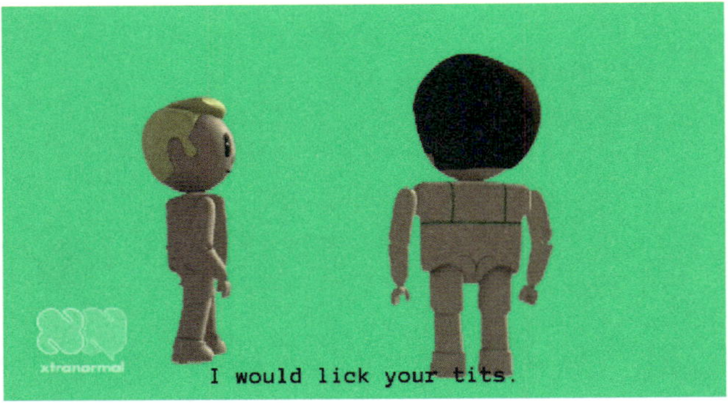
xtranormal
I would lick your tits.

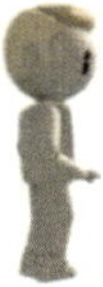

In the previous episode, after several weeks of sporadic virtual relations, the man finally told the woman his first name. It was Marcello, "like the great Mastrioanni." He urged her to watch Fellini's 8 1/2.

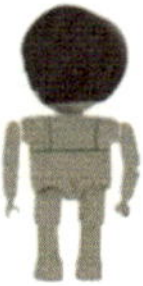

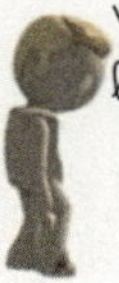

They spoke of collaborating. Marcello said: "I think that from sexual attraction can be born an idea." The woman agreed. He asked if she would like to see his best thing; she would.

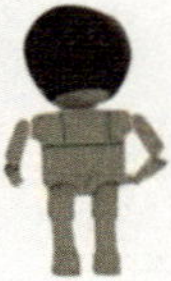

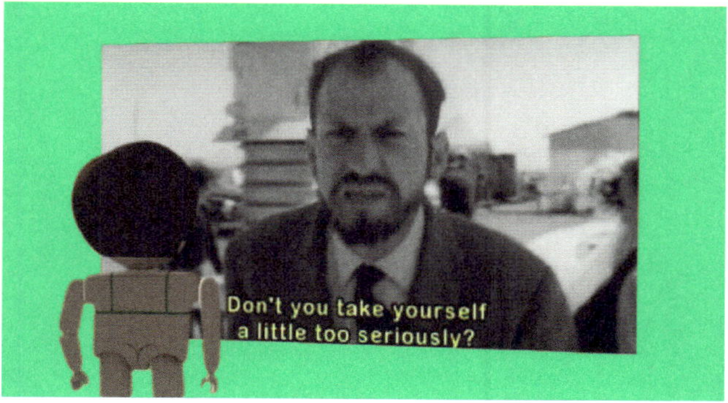
Don't you take yourself
a little too seriously?

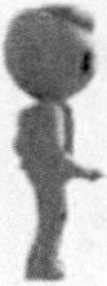

In the previous episode, a woman watched a scene from Fellini's 8 1/2 recommended to her by a semi-anonymous Italian filmmaker with whom she'd been having virtual relations for some months and with whom she'd been half-seriously discussing a collaborative experiment.

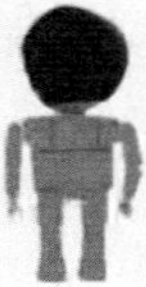

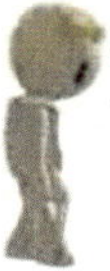

She told him he made her feel like she was watching a Godard film. She expressed adoration which he deflected with reasons why she shouldn't like him, e.g. "Remember Mickey Mouse? I have raped him!"

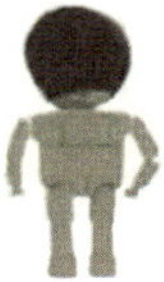

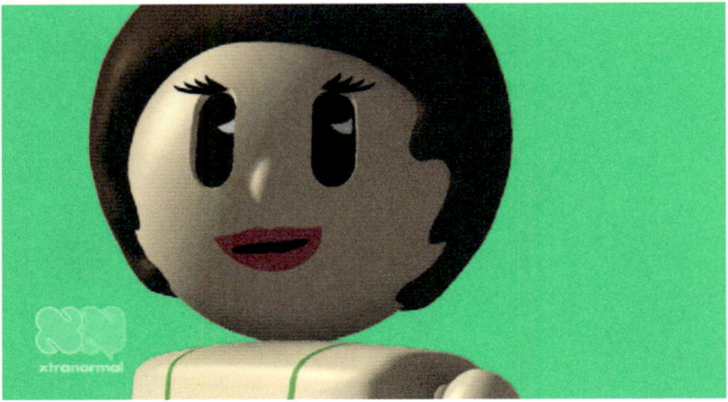
xtranormal

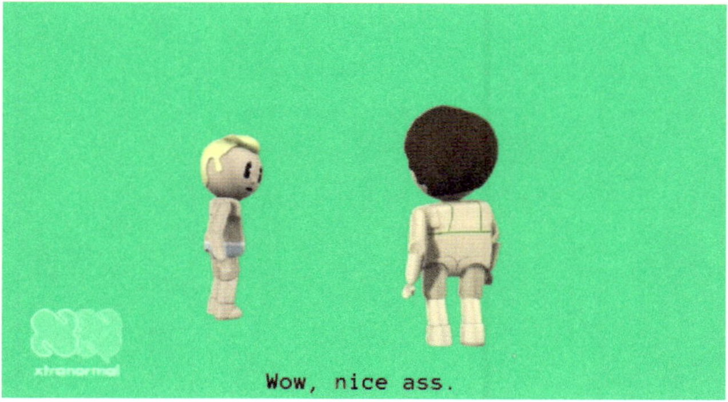
xtranormal
Wow, nice ass.

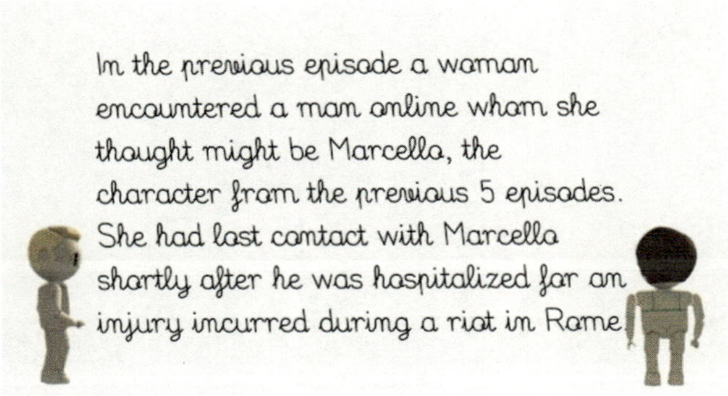
In the previous episode a woman encountered a man online whom she thought might be Marcello, the character from the previous 5 episodes. She had lost contact with Marcello shortly after he was hospitalized for an injury incurred during a riot in Rome

A self-described "multi-tasking man," Marcello was always working on many films and videos at once. The woman learned that this new man is not in fact Marcello, but a "degenerate son of artists" who is "the laziest man you'll ever meet."

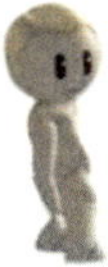

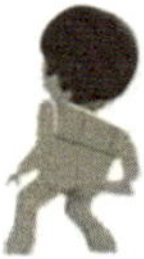

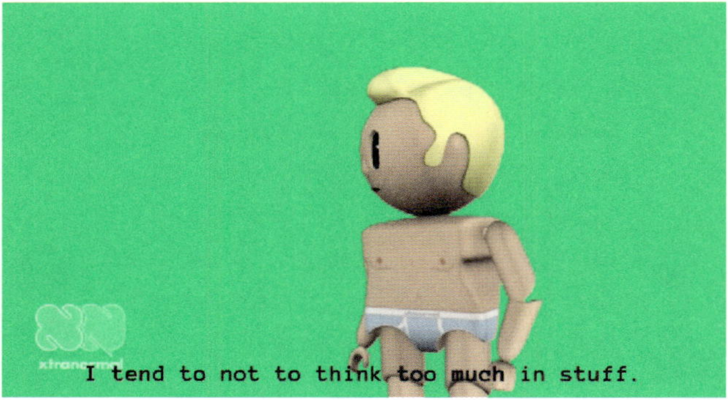
I tend to not to think too much in stuff.

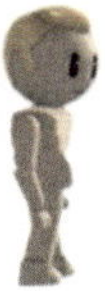

He told her he was once in Venice with his father who won a prize in the film festival, and that one of his father's films was conceptually extreme and scandalous. She told him about the novel Infinite Jest because one of its characters has a father who makes conceptually outlandish films.

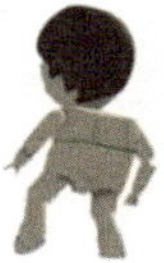

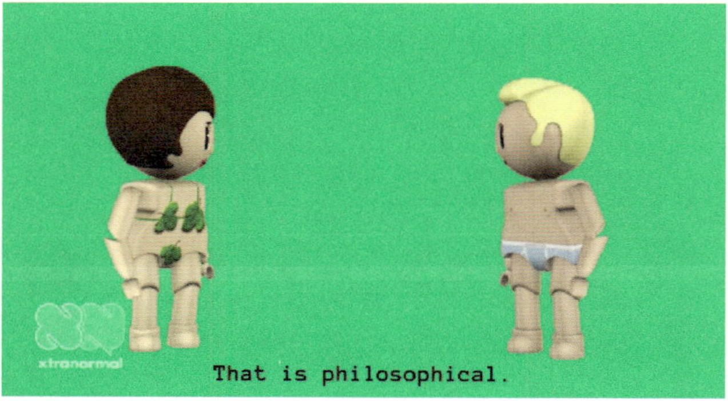
xtranormal
That is philosophical.

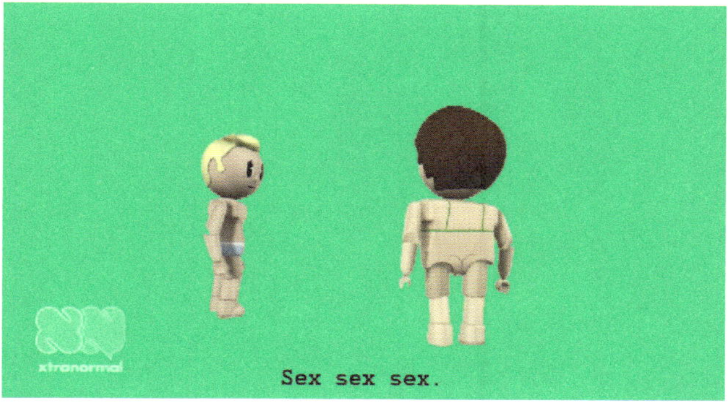
xtranormal
Sex sex sex.

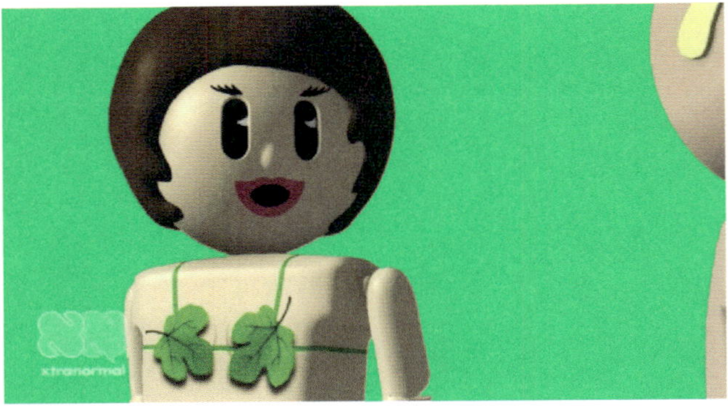
xtranormal

She initially pursued the bored guy because she mistook him for the best thing guy, but now wanted to put him in the film too. He told her he didn't want that, but later changed his mind.

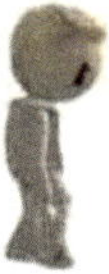

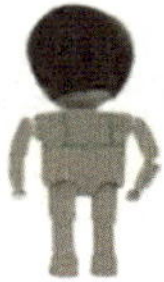

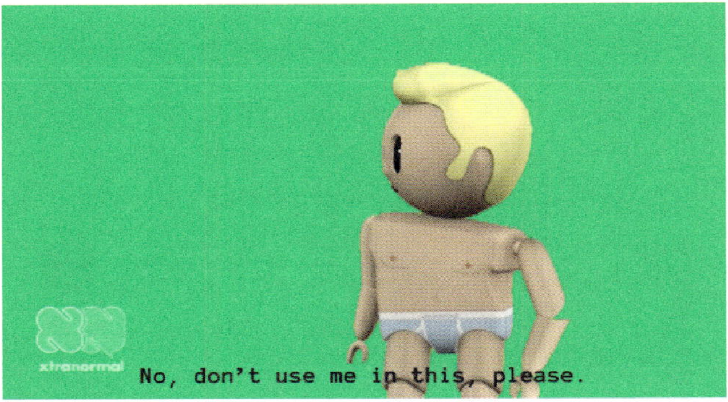
xtranormal
No, don’t use me in this, please.

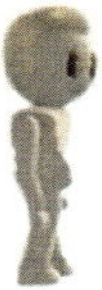

He explained how one of his father's films troubled him in the way it blurred the boundaries between fictional and real characters. They talked a lot about paying and receiving attention. They discussed certain writers. He asked, "Why do they all kill themselves?"

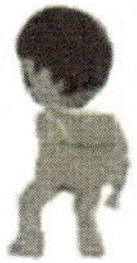

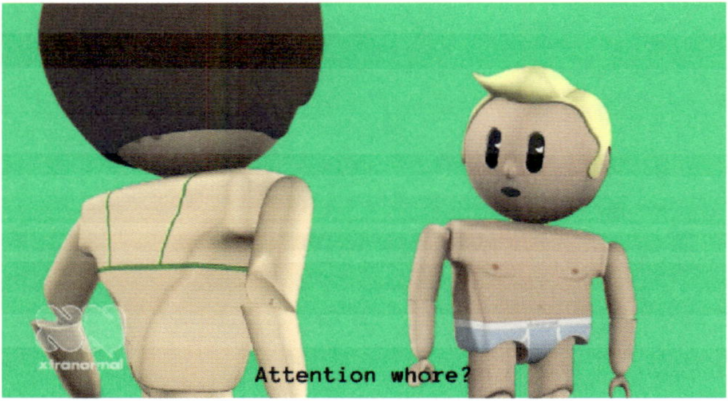
Attention whore?

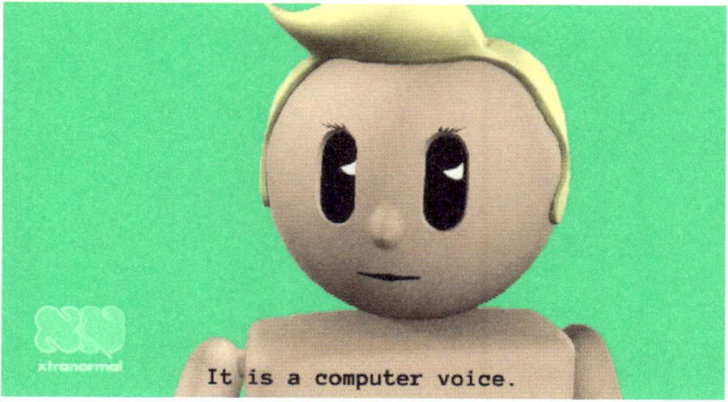
xtranormal
It is a computer voice.

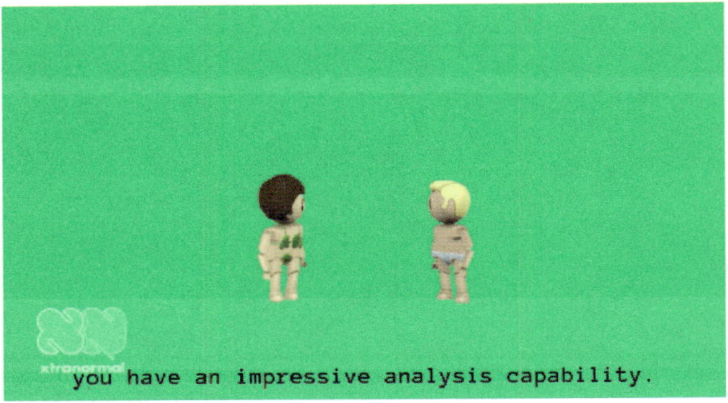
xtranormal
you have an impressive analysis capability.

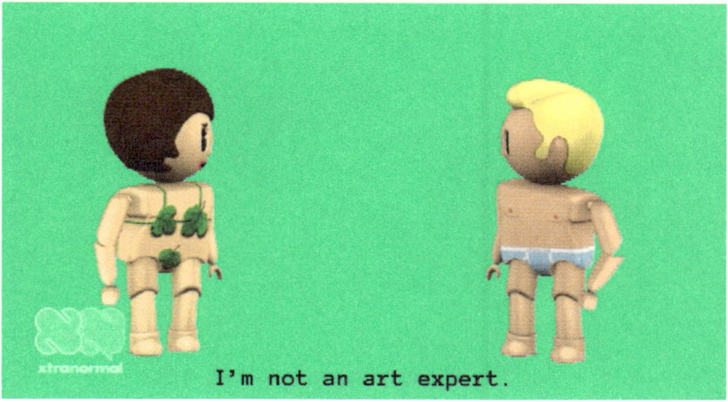
xtranormal
I'm not an art expert.

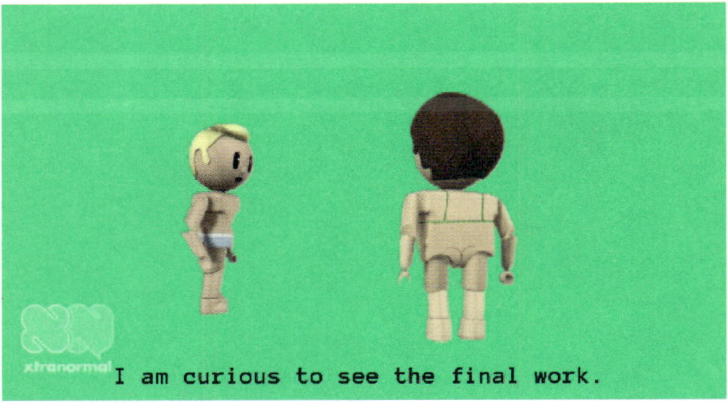
xtranormal
I am curious to see the final work.

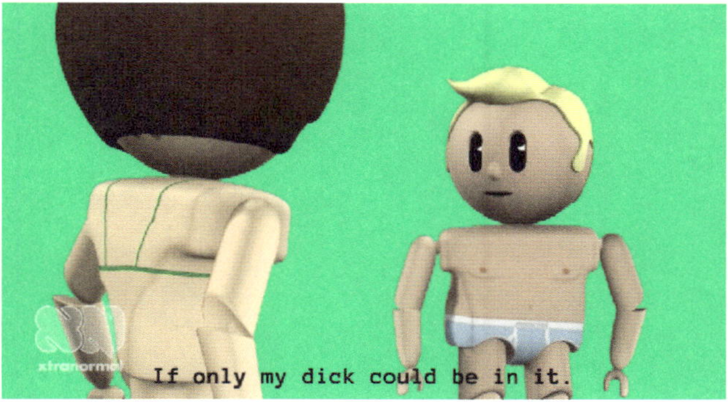
xtranormal
If only my dick could be in it.

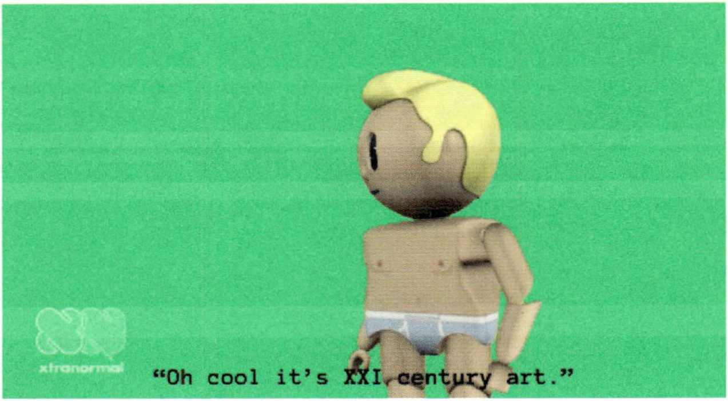
xtranormal
"Oh cool it's XXI century art."

Twenty-First Century Art
by Mark Godfrey

Chapter 1: The Plot

Frances Stark's *My Best Thing*, made for and first shown at the Venice Biennale in the Summer of 2011, is a single-channel projected animation that plays continuously for 99 minutes. It is broken into ten-and-a-half episodes of varying lengths. This essay adopts its structure from the animation addressing, in ten-and-a-half chapters, the various ideas raised by the work. First off, however, a plot summary in the expectation that this text will be read by some people who have not sat through the whole animation. (Dare I say it, even many of the people who claimed it was their favorite work of the Biennale did not watch it in its entirety. Stark anticipated and addressed the problem of attention spans, as we shall see.)

The animation begins with two characters, one a rudimentary 'female' and the other a 'male', preparing for and then engaging in a session of cam-sex. After orgasms, the girl sends the boy a video clip from a Beenie Man video and explains her recent obsession with dancehall music. She also lets him know that she has been invited to participate in the Venice Biennale. The boy assumes this is the cinema biennale and the girl corrects him before her phone rings (with a dancehall ringtone) and the episode ends. Their conversation continues in the second episode, during which she explains that she has begun to think about making art related to her virtual sex experiences. The boy reveals his name as Marcello and asks her if she has seen Fellini's *8 ½*. In the next episode (numbered 2 ½, in honor of its subject) the girl watches the climax of the film – the scene where the director Guido, played by Marcello Mastroianni, shoots himself underneath the table set up on his film-set where he is supposed to give a press conference. In episode three, the conversation and cam-sex resumes. The girl has been asking Marcello (who is a film-maker) if he would consider collaborating with her for her Venice project, but he explains that he might not be let into the States because of possible connections to terrorist activities. The girl does not take this seriously at first, and so the boy sends her a clip of recent political riots in Greece, which he introduces as 'poetry'. The fifth episode opens with the girl, alone, searching for the boy, eventually finding him and hearing disturbing news: the boy has been the victim of police brutality, and has suffered head injuries. He now faces trial – any plans to visit and collaborate with the girl are now impossible.

As the sixth episode begins, the 'boy' has changed appearance: he now wears underpants instead of a fig-leaf. The girl has mistaken him for Marcello but realizes this is another person. The pair has some sex despite the girl being late for her teaching job. She tells him about the impending Venice project and he too wrongly assumes she is talking about the cinema biennale – an event he is familiar with, because his parents are film-makers. In the seventh episode, the girl explains her intention to turn the narrative of the first five episodes into an art work, and the difficulties in doing this, given the limited attention of visitors to the Biennale. Another session of cam-sex occurs in the eighth episode after a discussion of the messiness of the girl's studio, and after this, the conversation takes different paths, some to do with the girl's ongoing work on her piece for Venice, some to do with writers and philosophers including Jacques Rancière, Ludwig Wittgenstein, Robert Walser, David Foster Wallace, and Thomas Bernhard. The ninth episode finds the boy distracted, checking through several chat sites rather than concentrating on the conversation with the girl – and this upsets her – but they continue to discuss literature and philosophy, and the challenges she faces as she assembles her new work. At the end of this episode the boy wonders why so many writers that they have discussed "kill themselves", a question which, as the girl reveals in the final episode, has brought her to tears. She continues to describe the processes of making her new work, and reflects on her situation as an artist, confessing her "pathological openness" and that she can seem "an attention whore", but also defensive and proud of the work she makes. She explains why she sees masturbation and art-making as connected. Both are forms of waste, and as such are forms of resistance in a world governed by ideals of efficiency and productivity. The boy lays waste to her defense, and the work ends.

When she decided to make an art work based on this narrative, Stark's first decision was to represent experiences and conversations between real people (exchanges mediated by webcams, microphones, speakers, keyboards and screens) using animated avatars close to those we know from computer games and online environments (for example, Wii's Miis). She could have represented the experiences and conversations in many other ways – directing actors, for instance, or incorporating the text of the conversations into drawings or powerpoints, media she has used in previous works. The avatars put considerable distance between the artwork and the actual events on which the dialogues are based. But of course this distance only serves to make us think about the absent and real bodies more intensely. We ask serious questions about the status of the actual body today – the desiring body, the aging body – and how our bodies are coping with increasingly mediated encounters (through Skype, messaging, and so on). We also think about how technologies are creating and enabling desires: for instance, how Skype gives some of its users who are in monogamous relationships permission to have web-sex with strangers without this activity necessarily being construed as infidelity.

As for how to create these avatars, Stark discovered free animation software called Xtranormal. On the Xtranormal site, anyone can select characters, choose their accents, select the backgrounds against which they appear, type in conversation, and then play with the 'camera angles' as if editing footage taken of the characters from a range of viewpoints. The characters in *My Best Thing* have very limited movements, which means that they cannot simulate the activities of the real people on whom they are based: the Xtranormal characters do not undress for one another, they do not masturbate, they do not type into keyboards, shut doors, or adjust webcams. Instead, they stand up, at some distance to each other, and talk. They have basic facial expressions and movements like blinking and smiling. Sometimes they dance. The characters' rather mundane activities contrast the sexual bodily acts of the real people that they stand in for, giving the work one of its most absurd qualities.

If you visit the Xtranormal site, you can see quickly how easily an animation like this is can be made, but you also get a good sense of Stark's other choices. She could have recreated the dialogues using more complex-looking figures, and she could have chosen more sophisticated backdrops for the scenes. Instead, she chose as basic a look for the animation as possible: the characters are two Playmobil figures in fig-leafs, and they appear against the most abstract of backgrounds: a green monochrome plane. Stark selected her characters and background from a menu with a limited range of choices, and the effect of these choices is complex. The animated figures recall both children's toys and Adam and Eve. The toy reference is funny, given the very adult nature of the dialogue. The biblical reference is more complex, especially when we consider that the figures are kitted-out in post-Fall costume.[1] A world of unrestricted round-the-clock sex might seem like a kind of paradise, yet these characters are clothed as if on the verge of their expulsion from Eden. This is quite appropriate in terms of the narrative of the animation, which starts with sex, and leads to one figure disappearing into possible captivity. A fall from paradise indeed.

As for the green screen – this seems at first to stand for the most abstracted 'natural' background, a basic Edenic setting for Adam and Eve. But it ends up recalling the green screens of Hollywood studios. The green screen is a non-place where an actor's body is suspended: their location is undetermined, to be defined at a later date, when they are long gone. The idea of the green screen fits the content of *My Best Thing*, where bodies have lost their moorings. The girl figure is connected to Los Angeles, the boys to Italy. They talk about meeting up but cannot figure where and when to do so. They lose each other. The green screen gets across something of the sense of lost-ness that accompanies their experience.

Chapter 3: "and it's all true"

So far I have refrained from calling the 'girl' character 'Frances'. It would be crude and simple to conflate the Playmobil girl with the artist Frances Stark, and to assume that every word the character utters was once said, or typed, by Frances Stark. *My Best Thing* is highly mediated, the end result of months of crafting and editing. It is about mediation, and it is not a direct document of conversations that took place. However, it would also be wrong to ignore as irrelevant the question of whether the animated events were based on actual events that involved Stark and men she met on the internet. Indeed the animation provokes its viewers to wonder about its relationship to actual encounters involved in making the work, mainly because it contains so much material referring to the actual encounter of the viewer, watching the work. When I saw the piece in Venice, hearing about the Playmobil girl's struggles to complete a work for the Biennale, I could not help but also wonder if the other parts of the work were also based on past events, especially since the 'Frances' character insists, while explaining the story of the first Italian to the second, that "it's all true".

There are two reasons why it should be of consequence whether the animation has a factual basis. We have all heard of the scenario of older men and women entering internet chatrooms, and lying about their identity as they converse with the younger participants. The scenario is such a cliché that it becomes the source of a joke for Marcello, who in the fourth episode of *My Best Thing*, claims to reveal himself as a "seventy-six year old Israelian", a revelation we understand as a joke. We also know that gamers in environments such as Second Life use avatars to create new identities that are distant from their everyday selves. If the avatars and their conversations in

My Best Thing are not so far removed from actual people and events, this would mean that Stark has used a form with strong associations to fiction and even to deception and self-deception, in a work which actually has a factual basis. We might also point to the distance between the 'Frances' avatar of *My Best Thing* and the most famous art-avatar to this date, Ann Lee. Pierre Huyghe and Philippe Parreno were interested in using the manga girl precisely because it was a figure without a character, one whose identity could change as each artist adapted it to make a work. Where Ann Lee had no fixed identity, Stark's avatars have identities pretty close to Frances Stark and her internet companions.

The second reason why it is interesting that the animation might have a basis in actual events is that this would mean that Frances Stark, a successful artist, and Professor of Painting and Drawing at the University of South California, has revealed herself to be an internet sex addict, or at least someone who is as likely to be found in her studio masturbating to webcam images of young Italian men as she is to be creating art works. This is quite a radical disclosure and even a brave one: many women artists have made works about sexual desire, but it is still unusual for an artist to be so explicit about desire, especially when she also is clear within her work about being a mother, the partner of a long-term boyfriend, and so on. Stark reveals that these day-to-day relationships leave her wanting more and that (at a period in her life when she might be expected to be satisfied with her domestic situation) she is actively seeking new and different sexual experiences. There is absolutely nothing unusual about this, but it is unusual for this to become the basis of an art work.

Chapter 4: Laughter and Language

The humor of *My Best Thing* is pretty irresistible. At the risk of laboring the point, it is hilarious to see web-sex simulated by Playmobil figures doing nothing with their cartoon hands and genitals (which are concealed anyway), and just standing around gasping "MMM". Stark squeezes as many laughs as she can from the absurdities of web-sex: foreplay is interrupted time and time again by broken connections, malfunctioning webcams, noisy keyboards, frozen screens, faulty microphones and by pop-up windows appearing on the participants' screens to distract them (the second boy realizes he has won an internet poker-game at one point). One might place *My Best Thing* at the end of a line of conceptual and postconceptual art works which replace erotic sexual acts and images with absurd ones: beginning with Dan Graham's *Detumescence*, 1966, a text piece describing "in clinical language the typical emotional and physiological aspects of post-climax in the sexual experience of the human male",[2] this mini-tradition flourished in Stark's homestate: think of Ed Ruscha's *Crackers*, 1969, a photo-novel showing Ruscha preparing a salad in a hotel bedroom, leaving to pick up his date, and then taking her back to the hotel where she undresses, lies on the lettuce leaves, and gets covered by salad dressing; John Baldessari's *Imagine This Woman…*, 1973, a sequence of seven identical images of a naked blonde, presumably appropriated from *Playboy*, each with a text instruction underneath asking the viewer to imagine her "unsightly", "blemished", and so on; Douglas Huebler's *Variable Piece 70 (Blue Series 90F)*, 1974, for which Huebler took a number of porn images, cropped the faces, and captioned them with a text suggesting that the photos show "at least one person who might feel extremely embarrassed if his, or her mother were ever to see the whole picture." Think also of Ilene Segalove's 1974 *Nine Purple Packages*, a grid of nine self-portraits in which the artist appears in the identical low-cut purple v-neck: she stares to the camera, but we are forced to stare at her chest, because the only difference in the images is that she wears a different bra in each. More recently, think of Mike Kelley's *Missing Time Color Exercise* series, 1998, for which Kelley took a number of covers of the cartoon magazine *Sex to Sexty* and arranged them according to the prevailing tone of the cover as if to create a color chart, at the same time replacing the missing issues in the run with monochrome panels of the missing colors, and most recently, Christopher Williams' photographs of socks, kinky shoes, and models-in-brassieres, their moles and foot-corns present and un-airbrushed.

Back to *My Best Thing*: the treatment of spoken and written language in the work is also very funny. Xtranormal allows the user to choose from a range of accents: Stark selected an American female voice to speak the girl's words, and Italian male voice to speak the boy's. The American woman sounds suave and well-educated. Hers is the kind of voice that might be used in a tasteful TV ad, which makes lines like "I wish I could take it out and put it in my mouth now" all the more amusing. The Italian accent is by contrast extremely crude, computerized, and caricatured and becomes even funnier because the words are accompanied by subtitles, and because the Italian characters so often make basic phrasing mistakes such as "we cum together less or more". Stark also has her characters annunciate acronyms that are meant for text only, like LOL. (Another of my favorite Los Angelean comedians, Larry David, built an episode of *Curb Your Enthusiasm* around the same conceit: a character responds to Larry's joke by saying "LOL" and Larry later has the job of telling her to stop saying this acronym for 'Laugh out loud' out-loud.)

Language is a source of humor in *My Best Thing* but it also becomes a very important political subject. During the dialogues, it becomes evident that the Italian feels pretty angered by the hegemony of the English language, which is not only the dominant language of the internet, but the language of globalized capitalism. "English is useful, Italian, not", he complains, and later realizes that he simply cannot express his philosophical ideas in English, which means that the sophistication of his thought will not be clear to his new internet partner. She encourages him to use Google Translate and he quickly replies that "Google translate can produce war". Later, joking, he calls her "Fucking American girl that doesn't speak Esperanto because she thinks English is the best". The 'real' Frances Stark seems to acknowledge the accusation and even opened herself up to further criticism by premiering the work in Italy without any Italian subtitles. English is the dominant language of the art world too, even when the art world visits Italy: Stark points to the problem of this situation while knowing she can do little to change it.

Chapter 5: Show me your face

'My Best Thing' is Marcello's nickname for his penis, and the nickname is another cause for laughter in the video that is named after this moniker. "Want to see my best thing?" he asks. The girl does, but she also wants to see his face. "Will you show me your face, your whole face, I want to see the pleasure on your face?"

Given the readiness of both characters to display their sex-organs to each other, and the usual associations of 'facial' in the world of internet sex, this request is one of the most tender moments of the work. Seeing someone's face is normally the basis for sexual attraction and precedes any sexual contact; in the world of internet web-sex, however, exposing your face carries the risks of exposing your identity, and leaves you vulnerable in other ways.

Stark once quoted from Emily Dickinson's poem "A Charm invests a face / Imperfectly beheld / A Lady dare not lift her Veil / For fear it be dispelled." She added "I still a fetching face would like / to match up to my wits".[3] In *My Best Thing* it is the boy who wants to keep on his 'veil' (Marcello hides his face from his web-cam) but the girl is still worried that her face might not be cute enough, not young enough to sustain his attraction. Given all this, the moment where the dialogue suggests that the characters have exposed their faces is monumental. For Emmanuel Levinas, the face became a way of thinking about the beginnings of an ethical relationship between self and Other: "The epiphany of the face is ethical."[4] To encounter the face was to encounter the vulnerability of another person, and one's own vulnerability too: "There is first the very uprightness of the face, its upright exposure, without defence."[5]

Chapter 6: gimmie gimmie gimmie

Just after the girl has asked to see the boy's face, she sends him a link to a Beenie Man video for his song *Gimmie Gimmie Gimmie* and explains that she is in "a serious dancehall phase." We are still within the first episode of *My Best Thing* and already we are confronted with a whole new set of problems. Beenie Man was famously barred from performing in the UK, the Netherlands, New Zealand and elsewhere after lyrics such as "I'm dreaming of a new

Jamaica, come to execute all the gays" led to the murder of homosexuals in his home country. In the video for *Gimmie Gimmie Gimmie*, the dancehall reggae superstar sits on a throne as a sequence of girls from "Trinidad and Bagdad, From Islamabad... and Masada" gyrate before him. He boasts of being a "pum pum gaad" (pum pum meaning vagina) and a "love god cah mi love pussy bad." "God mek woman", he continues, and "woman drive man mad."

Thomas Crow opened his famous essay 'Modernism and Mass Culture in the Visual Arts', by asking "What is to be made of the continuing involvement between modernist art and the materials of low or mass culture?"[6] But whatever it meant for Manet and Seurat to paint the bars and entertainment halls of Paris, for Picasso and Braque to incorporate printed material into their collages, for Rauschenberg and Warhol to silkscreen film-stars and non-stars onto canvas, or for Jeff Koons to turn children's inflatables and toy decorations into sculpture, something else is going on here. This isn't just high art attracted to 'mass culture' but to a cultural form which is apparently violently hostile to its values. Put simply: what does it mean for an artist to advertise her attraction to a musician and video that is so flagrantly misogynistic? How does one interpret this attraction alongside other aspects of Stark's work, for instance, her own characterization of the female artist as the 'housewife' as opposed to the male 'architect'?[7] How can one reconcile the unlikely bedfellows Beenie Man and Sylvia Sleigh, a feminist painter whose work appears in a recent work of Stark's and that the 'Frances' character describes to the Italian boy in *My Best Thing*? The Sleigh painting is *The Turkish Bath*, 1973 and features an array of nude men, arranged in a formation that quotes Ingres's 1862 *Turkish Bath*. If artists of Sleigh's generation labored to confront the sexism of old masters such as Ingres by producing their own accounts of desire, doesn't Beenie Man's video represent a regression to a moment where men can represent women as flesh-on-parade?

Of course there are no easy answers here, but the main point to stress is that these attractions of 'Frances's' character to Beenie Man and to Sylvia Sleigh, or to dancehall culture and to feminism, cannot be reconciled, because desire is not straightforward. We cannot be held accountable for our different attractions, and it is one of the most contemporary aspects of Stark's work that it resists being pious about desire and is honest about its contradictions. Maybe it's just the case that a woman artist can totally admire the work and politics of a feminist predecessor and at the same time be transfixed by the sexiness of the men and women in *Gimmie Gimmie Gimmie*, and that's that.

But is there not a more troubling question to be asked? Is Frances Stark, white Californian, attracted to black dancehall culture because it seems for her to be an arena of pure and primitive sexuality? Is 'Stark: dancehall' equivalent to 'Ingres: the harem', or 'Gauguin: Tahiti', or 'Matisse: Morocco'? Maybe the problem lies not so much with the homophobic, misogynist Beenie Man but with the neo-primitivist Frances Stark? We cannot escape these questions, and far from putting them to one side, after *My Best Thing*, Stark compounded them even more: *Put a Song in Your Thing*, her 2011 Performa event took her dancehall attraction as one of its main subjects, and included a screening of a dancehall video of daggering (a dance based on exaggerated and very rough sex), a meeting with a daggering star Skerrit Bwoy, and climaxed in Stark being daggered.

But to return to *My Best Thing*, perhaps the questions about primitivism can be complicated (if not set-aside entirely) if we entwine them with other questions raised by the work. First: if *My Best Thing* is about simulation and sex (the simulation of bodily sex by Stark and the Italian as they looked at each other on their screens; the simulation of this simulation by the Playmobil characters) then maybe the attraction to dancehall is that this is just another more convincing, funnier, and much sexier form of simulation – for Beenie Man is not actually fucking the girls who dance for him, but acting in a music video. And if *My Best Thing* is about the hegemony of English, is not Beenie Man a figure of resistance, because (unlike Marcello) he has found a way to invent a language using English as he sees fit, and to place this language, unapologetically, into the circuits of MTV and youtube? Finally, if Beenie Man presents himself in the video with a lineup of girls from all over the world, might Stark have been amused by the video because in her chatroom escapades she found herself in a similar position – with men from all over the world lining up for her in front of their webcams? Perhaps Stark (whose nickname is Beanie) was more intrigued by her connections to the dancehall star than by the obvious differences of sex and race.

Chapter 6½: 8½

In a kind of exchange of gifts, having received *Gimmie Gimmie Gimmie*, Marcello encourages 'Frances' to watch Fellini's *8 ½*. He thinks she might be interested in it, as it concerns a director's struggles to complete and film a new feature, while being pressured by producers, external script writers, and a range of actresses. 'Frances' stands watching it, transfixed.

The film was of course fascinating for Stark. While she identified with the way the director-character was constantly distracted from his work by his sexual encounters, *8 ½*'s main function in *My Best Thing* is to permit and open up a whole sequence of self-reflexive passages where the 'Frances' character considers her other problems in making her own work. She describes her anxieties preparing a work for a large audience on a tight deadline, the difficult conditions of display for this work, and the consequent challenges that viewers may face. She worries about how to condense and organize the narrative of her online encounters, and also how to hold people's attentions with a projected animation when (at the opening of Venice) they have so much else to see.

Like *8 ½*, *My Best Thing* therefore comes to be a work one of whose main 'themes' is art making, extending another rich tradition including Italo Calvino's novel *If On A Winter's Night A Traveler* and John Baldessari's *A Painting That is Its Own Documentation*, 1968 – present. *My Best Thing* also relates to other historical works about the pressures placed on artists to create, and here we can think of another Italian whose work has appeared within Stark's own recent paintings: Alighiero Boetti, who showed the artist as a torn and divided figure, expected to play the roles of a shaman – a private creator of art works – and a showman – a public figure, entertaining an audience with an increasing appetite for spectacle.

Because so many of its self-reflexive passages refer to the location of its premiere screening, the Venice Biennale, *My Best Thing* also marks a new moment in the history of site-specificity. The art historian Miwon Kwon has charted the history of this idea very clearly and shown how early site-specific works in which artists responded to the architectural and spatial conditions of display made way for later works where artists treated the site in terms of its economic and institutional identity: how was a site funded, how was it maintained, who else worked in it apart from the artist?[8] Stark was reflecting on the site of the Venice Biennale in a new way: she was not really concerned with the architecture of the pavilions and Arsenale, nor with the idea of a national pavilion (as have been recent artists such as Steve McQueen), nor with the funding structures of the Biennale and the institution's roles in the city: she took the site of the 'Venice Biennale' as a social and temporal entity, as a fixture (indeed *the* fixture) in the art world calendar, with attendant anxieties for artists and viewers alike. For the artist, Venice is a massive platform where they are exposed to countless critics, curators, gallerists, and fellow artists. For a viewer, when you go to Venice (especially for the opening) you find yourself surrounded by friends and colleagues from your profession, with too little time to socialize and to see all the art on display. Being there means experiencing a degree of anxiety about where you should be, what you should see, whom you should party with, and what unmissable shows you are missing. These are the affects I experience in Venice, and they are anticipated and thematized in *My Best Thing*, especially when 'Stark' complains about her Venice viewers being "distracted", and about the "unavoidable assumption that nobody can afford to pay attention."

Stark accurately describes the mode of attention and impatience of viewers bustling around Venice but also more generally she acknowledges the great problem faced by artists making durational work today: that their audience, too distracted by the pressures of contemporary life – by constant incoming emails and texts on smart phones and so on – are no longer able to concentrate on lengthy art works. Her genius move, in my opinion, was to attend to her distracted audience's needs by breaking her work into bite-size chunks but to stick to her intentions without compromise: this animation would last as long as it needed to. Those who only watched a few episodes might make a similar accusation to the one made in *8 ½* of Guido's film by his friend, a critic – that the work is "a chain of gratuitous episodes which may be amusing" yet lacking in "a central issue". Stark would run the risk of being criticized in such a way, knowing that anyone who did watch the work the whole way through would think otherwise.

Chapter 7: Poetry in the Streets

In the fourth episode of *My Best Thing*, Marcello begins to indicate that he has connections to radical groups in Italy. He explains to the girl that there was a moment of revolutionary activity in the country, referring to the *anni di piombo* in the 1970s, and hopes that "now, there are some reasons to believe it will come again. I think it is possible to happen a riot." The girl's immediate response is to make all of this safe by connecting it to her ideas of '68-era European culture: "I felt just now I was in a Godard film". However, Marcello refuses to let his activities be romanticized or associated with the past in this way, and sends her a clip of the riot that took place in Athens on 5 May 2010 in which police acted with extreme brutality towards crowds of protestors and a bank was attacked with Molotov cocktails, leading to three civilian deaths. Marcello announces the clip by writing "The poetry is this". These words operate in the opposite way to her line about Godard: he defines a riot as poetry, rather than connecting talk of a riot to a European film. His designation recalls Situationist graffiti from May 1968: "Poetry is in the streets". As outlined above, Marcello seems to disappear after this episode, and when he renews contact, he reveals that he has been beaten by police and faces a trial.

I have already considered *My Best Thing* as a site-specific work. In assessing its relationship to site, we also have to think about how this material worked in the context of the Venice Biennale. First we should remember that art-world visitors to the Biennale like to experience 'Italy' as a historic idyll: how pleasurable it is to consume art in the most beautiful city in the world, crammed with its *palazzi*, churches, and Bellini altarpieces. We also consume 'Italy' as we guzzle our free bellinis, prosciutto, and parmesan. The art should be contemporary, yes, but it shouldn't spoil the taste. Marcello jolts us from our reverie and confronts us with another Italy – an Italy of political chaos, economic catastrophe, and coming insurrection: by October, 2011, Rome experienced riots similar to those that we see in Athens.

Marcello's words also bring more troubled ideas about the body into *My Best Thing*: up to the point where he describes his injuries, we have been thinking about the desiring body, the embarrassed body, the aging body; and most of all the body as it is lived at a moment of technological history when so many daily activities are now mediated and do not involve our senses in the same way that they used to. With news of his injuries we confront a different idea of the body. Marcello's impending fate might be the one described in Giorgio Agamben's texts about the body of the 'homo sacer'. Unprotected by the law, and deprived of political and civil rights, all that is left is 'bare life'. During what he terms a 'state of exception', the state tends to treat its opponents this way.[9] A protestor's identity as a citizen with rights is set aside: they become a mere body, and a very vulnerable one.

Chapter 8: Why do they all kill themselves?

In the second half of *My Best Thing*, the discussions between 'Frances' and the second boy grow so complex that they begin to question whether it is odd "to have more thought than cam-sex with a virtual partner." The dialogue is so complete that there is very little to do here than summarize its main concerns: 'Frances' and the boy share reminiscences of reading Nietzsche for the first time, and she goes on to recommend to him Jacques Rancière's *The Ignorant Schoolmaster* with its critique of conventional pedagogy: in reading the book, she says, one becomes distrustful of the "tyranny of knowledge", and begins to understand that ignorance can be reframed as a position of potentiality, not as lack. The conversation moves on to David Foster Wallace's novel *Infinite Jest*. For 'Frances', the endless fascination in the novel with the unfinished avant-garde film mirrors her fascination with web-sex. With passing references to Wittgenstein and Picasso, the characters also discuss Robert Walser and Thomas Bernhard. They reflect on the horrific similarities of Foster Wallace's, Walser's, and Bernhard's deaths, and the boy asks "Why do they all kill themselves?" When 'Frances' persuades him to let her integrate the content of this conversation into the work she is making, she worries what a viewer might make of the combination of "suicide and random sex-chat?" He reassures her that they will think "cool, twenty-first century art". As I hope to have shown, the contemporaneity of *My Best Thing* is hardly restricted to this juxtaposition.

Chapter 9: Anti-Productivity

Towards the end of *My Best Thing*, the 'Frances' character and the second boy discuss whether the animation that is being developed from their conversations constitutes a "visual record of sex chat", a "reflection on a subject" or "art". She claims "a certain authorship status" and says that while she would not presume to say she makes "great art", she does defend that what she is making "is art". The boy says he was simply "raising the doubt" and she accepts this: raising the doubt is her "modus operandi", but one she needs to retreat from every now and then, because she is proud of what she makes, and likes talking about it, even to strangers. Given all this, we might expect that 'Frances' sees art as the valued outcome of her hard work but a few sentences later, she presents a very different idea: that art is somehow the opposite to work. "Maybe art is an opposite of working, in the sense that it is a form of resistance to productivity."

This claim marks Stark's distance from the generation of American artists in the late 1960s that began to present themselves as art workers, associating their labor with that of the working classes. There were important reasons for this identification but as Julia Bryan-Wilson shows in her recent book *Art Workers: Radical Practice in the Vietnam War Era*, sometimes artists were forced to realize that other workers were not so interested in aligning themselves with artists and their leftist causes.[10] The 'Frances' character's position is closer to another artist from this period whose work I have already mentioned – Boetti, who, in 1969, created a double of himself out of lumps of cement. Boetti titled the work *Me Sunbathing in Turin on 19 January 1969*: while everyone else in the city was busy manufacturing the products that created the 'economic miracle', Boetti was slacking, sunbathing. Later in the year, Boetti embarked on a series of drawings made on grid paper, the idea for which was to cover every line in the grid. The simplest way of covering all the lines would be to run the pencil up the verticals and along the horizontals, mimicking the way in which the original lines for the printed grid had been marked out. However, this would copy what he called "entirely bourgeois behavioural patterns" and would mean completing the task in "the quickest and more rational way": for Boetti such an approach had "nothing to do with being an artist". Instead of efficiency, Boetti pursued wastefulness, filling the grid up gradually, spending much more time than was needed merely to complete the task.[11]

This moment in Boetti's work recalls Georges Bataille's arguments about waste in *The Accursed Share*, ideas that have also surfaced in Stark's work, through the appearance of Avital Ronell's book *Crack Wars* in Stark's powerpoint projection *Structures That Fit My Opening And Other Parts Considered In Relation To Their Whole*, 2007. In the work, Stark presents pages and quotes from Ronell's book, one of which is a theorization, through Bataille, of the figure of the drug-addict. "Being-on-drugs resists the production of value which, on another, more Bataillean register, indicates that it disrupts the production of meaning."[12] *My Best Thing* is not the first time Stark has thought about non-productivity and art as not-working. These thoughts run through her practice: consider the way the studio is represented in her drawings. But what makes *My Best Thing* new is that it marks the first time that she has thought about anti-productivity as a principle underlining both art and masturbation: the full line quoted just now reads "Maybe art is an opposite of working, in the sense that it is a form of resistance to productivity as is masturbation, wasted seed." Many ideas were put forward throughout the twentieth century to deflate the idea of fine art, to deny the association between art and hard work or technical skill, and to associate art with the everyday or even with 'spit', from Duchamp's readymade through Bataille's *informe* and beyond, but this claim is something else.

Chapter 10: Can a Relationship between Two Persons be made in this way?

My Best Thing almost ends twice before its actual ending: the first false ending is the disappearance of Marcello; the second is the moment when the second boy asks "Why do they all kill themselves?" The actual ending comes after he lays waste to 'Frances's' arguments about masturbation-as-waste being a form of resistance to capitalist productivity: he says you produce juices, and "most of it goes down the toilet". It is a rather dystopian ending, this vision of a cum-soaked tissue being flushed away. But it should not dampen our appreciation of *My Best Thing*, which is in the final assessment, the most optimistic of twenty-first century artworks.

In order to understand the optimistic force of the work, I want (in conclusion) to set it in four new contexts. The first is an art-world context, namely the phenomenon of 'Relational Aesthetics'. Claire Bishop has criticized the environments created by artists such as Rirkrit Tiravanija as fostering a "cozy" and "feel-good" notion of the social.[13] In *My Best Thing* we have a much grittier and more substantial representation of what it means for strangers to meet: they come together (in both senses) and then begin substantial discussions. The second context for *My Best Thing* is the proliferation in the past few years of social networking sites such as Facebook, through which the world of commerce is able to penetrate social life, a realm previously outside the grip of capitalist command. Most social media sites collect the information we pass to our friends, and use this to enable advertisers to target us with pinpoint accuracy as potential customers. Brands, products, shops, and corporations become our 'friends'; we 'like' them and 'share' our approval. Just at the very point, thanks to the internet, when social life seems to have become colonized by capitalism, Stark presents an alternative, and no more clearly than when 'Marcello' shares his video from the Greek riots.

The next context for *My Best Thing* is precisely the sites that Stark visited in making it – sites such as Chatroulette which enable viewers to watch and play with each other naked. These sites might seem to be a sliver of the internet still outside the reach of commerce, but if one spends a few minutes on them, they seem to present an endless sequence of bored young people (mostly males) rubbing themselves. It is a rather gloomy vision of global anomie. *My Best Thing* shows that behind the look of dejection, these individuals have different stories, motivations, different frustrations with the world they have inherited, and different dreams too. The final context for *My Best Thing* is simply Steve McQueen's most recent feature, *Shame*, the other work made by a major artist in 2011 aiming to ask questions about sex today (this one did premiere at the 2011 Venice Film Festival).[14]

McQueen's film also probes how the internet has created new sexual behavior: it centers on a sex-addict imprisoned in his daily rituals of internet porn, incessant masturbation, chatrooms, and prostitutes. He finds emotional intimacy impossible, and while living in New York and going to work by day and bars by night, has withdrawn into a secretive and very solitary world that seems more desolate with each new sexual partner. *Shame* does not present itself as a cautionary tale about the dangers of the internet, as it is specifically about its central character and his addiction, yet it does stand in very sharp contrast to *My Best Thing*, which is all about the possibility of emotional intimacy, not its destruction.

To return one more time to *My Best Thing*: the relationships between 'Frances' and the two men might have begun because people separated by huge distances and a nine hour time gap were simultaneously looking for someone to masturbate with, but they end up being tender, caring, complex, thoughtful, and loving. 'Stark' is moved several times: "you had me falling in love". "That made me cry".... Gradually, as we watch the animation, a utopian vision of the social emerges. Strangers meet, communicate, share ideas rather than brand preferences, and change how each one sees the world. It is extremely precarious, because at any minute a technical glitch might occur and the conversation could end. But maybe this is a new Eden after all.

1 A precursor for Stark's project is Francis Picabia's 1924 *Ciné-Sketch*. This was 'a sex-farce performed in a staccato style' and included 'a nude, bearded Duchamp and the artist's model Brogna Perlmütter as Lucas Cranach's Adam and Eve'. Man Ray took a photograph of the pair. See Katie-Croll Knight, 'Chronology' in Jennifer Mundy (ed.), *Man Ray – Duchamp – Picabia* (Tate Modern, London, 2008) p. 198. Thanks to Kitty Scott for reminding me about Man Ray's photograph.

2 Dan Graham, 'Detumescence' in *Dan Graham: Works 1965–2000* (Museu de Arte Contemporanea de Serralves, Porto, 2001) p.98.

3 Frances Stark, 'Three Works', *Fama & Fortune Bulletin,* P&S Wien, 1997, unpaginated.

4 Emmanuel Levinas, *Totality and Infinity*, trans. Alphonso Lingis (Pittsburgh: Duquesne University Press, 2000) p. 197.

5 Emmanuel Levinas, *Ethics and Infinity*, trans. Richard A. Cohen (Pittsburgh: Duquesne University Press, 1999) p. 86.

6 Thomas Crow, *Modern Art in the Common Culture* (Yale University Press, New Haven and London, 1996) p.3.

7 Frances Stark, *The Architect & The Housewife* (Bookworks, London, 1999).

8 Miwon Kwon, *One Place after Another: Site-specific Art and Locational Identity* (The MIT Press, Cambridge, Mass., 2002).

9 Giorgio Agamben, *Homo Sacer: Sovereign Power and Bare Life*, trans. Daniel Heller-Roazen (Stanford University Press, Stanford, 1998) and *State of Exception*, trans. Kevin Attell (The University of Chicago Press, Chicago and London, 2005).

10 Julia Bryan-Wilson, *Art Workers: Radical Pracice in the Vietnam War Era* (University of Chicago Press, Chicago, 2009).

11 Mark Godfrey, *Alighiero E Boetti* (Yale University Press, New Haven and London, 2011).

12 Avitall Ronell quoted by Frances Stark. See *Frances Stark: Collected Works* (Van Abbemuseum, Eindhoven, 2007) p. 116.

13 Claire Bishop, 'Antagonism and Relational Aesthetics', *October* 110, (Fall 2004), p. 79.

14 McQueen has said "I wanted to try to make a film about what's going on now… a film that reflects reality". Steve McQueen in conversation with Stuart Comer, Tate Modern, London, 12 December 2011.

Episode 9

Female So, your mother is out of town tonight? And you are alone?

Male Yep. Until Friday or Saturday.

F Oh great.

M Wow. You sent me an email about my father.

F That is what I asked about earlier, if it was ok, you said it was. Hmm, my guess is you are just reading it now.

M Haha. I am not that sexy. I am afraid the webcam is giving you the wrong impression.

F I could say the same.

M No, you look sexy.

F Aw, you should be more confident.

F So, what are you doing right now?

M Just chatting. MSN. Facebook. Chatroulette. Cigarettes. TV.

F Jesus.

M Haha. What?

F Here is some woman you think is sexy, being nice to you, trying to amuse you, and you still are searching for another on Chatroulette?

M Haha.I am not searching. I am just on it. If a sexy girl comes along, who am I not to reply?

F Well I'll let you go then, bye.

M Oh, no. You are jealous?

F I don't think that's the word.

M What is the word then? You are pissed off.

F No. I'm just embarrassed for giving you attention and you don't feel like giving it back.

M I see. But opening windows does not mean I am not giving you attention. I have it all on, but mostly I am chatting with you.

M Oh my god. What a news… Two police officers in L.A. were caught doing a porn movie.

F Hahahaha.

M A black police officer and a hot blonde girl.

F I know those guys.

M You do? LOL.

F Hahaha, just kidding.

M Haha.

F Well, hm, I'm feeling a bit sad now.

M Why?

F Because the LAPD has lost its moral compass. Haha. No.

M I think it's more than understandable. She's hot and blonde. He's black. Let's do a porn movie while we are working.

F So, how do you feel about me calling you 'spiritually bored'?

M You called me that? LOL.

F Oh Jesus.

M Haha.

F I'm really barking up the wrong tree. Hahahahaha.

M LOL. Wait. I will read it.

M Well, you have an impressive analysis capability. What can I say?

F So I shouldn't be surprised that someone who I know to be extraordinarily ambivalent isn't paying close enough attention to me. Hahahaha.

M LOL. I think the fact that I am not speaking my native language makes a difference.

F Yes and no.

M It may be a mechanism to economize the cognitive effort.

F Hahahahahahaha.

M Solid argument.

F Haha. I was thinking, why would I spend energy on you, who I know are kind of indifferent, not particularly passionate, etc.

M Yes.

F And I was trying to understand this mysterious fixation. And I felt that somehow I...

M Because I have a nice cock?

F Well, you certainly do.

M LOL.

F But, hey, I see a lot of nice cocks, so that's not it.

M Oh, damn.

F I thought that maybe you were currently in a holding pattern in your life.

M A holding pattern in my life? What does that mean? Like I'm waiting to know what I'll do with it?

F Yeah.

M Yes it's true. And it bothers me to think about it.

F And I thought somehow I could crack you open. And it would put something into play for you.

M Perhaps.

F I really felt this. I know it sounds a bit deluded but...

M So your fantasy is that you'll somehow be a master to a lost soul?

F Haha. Well I have never thought of it in those terms.

M It fits the picture.

F Your anomie is palpable. Can you Google-translate that?

M I think I understood it. Lack of rules.

F It also means aimless and disaffected.

M Yes, maybe it's a psychological issue. Maybe it's my essence to be slightly indifferent. But I also get disgusted with people who are too much like that.

F Maybe it is, and yes, I appreciate that paradox.

M I need to go outside.

F Interesting timing, haha.

M It's a nice night. It's my routine If you are here when I get back, we'll chat some more. I almost always go out at this hour. At least to the café to see my friends…

F Okay. Well I would love to see you while you are alone in the house.

M Okay, if you are online when I come back…

M Hey, I'm back. Are you back to work?

F I'm not back to work because I am somehow always here.

M Where?

F Here in this chair, at this table, with my laptop trying to pull this story together. I would like to try to use this story with you, so would you like to pick a name for yourself?

M If you are using me as a character, I don't want to have anything to do with that.

M In one of my father's films, the main character was my father, and he had a son in the movie, and it was a bit confusing to me. Even though I knew it was just a movie. What happened in the film was close to what was happening in real life. Something very difficult.

F I read about it, it seems very intense.

M It was moving. It was. But it was very very weird to me to live the bad thing two times.

F I think artists cannot help from being inconsiderate of people, even people they love, in order to do what they think they need to do. I can really understand why your father did that. But sorry, I know nothing so I shouldn't talk.

M It's okay.

F But you are over the movie now?

M Yes, completely. I like the movie. I laughed my brains out when I read the script. Very well written. Very, very well written.

F Wow. So nice.

M There is a student who's writing about my father's work. I was with him at the house where all the things that belonged to my father are. Sorry for the bad English.

F No, no, I understand everything.

M So I was there listening to the Goldberg Variations while he sorted the CDs.

F Oh my. That is such a curious thing. My boyfriend was once re-publishing this guy's work and he had gone out to the house, where there was the daughter. She brought a box of things and he got to photocopy it. He showed them to me and I fell in love with the guy.

M LOL.

F One of my favorite books is about this guy who has to take responsibility for pulling together all the work of a dead friend. And the guy's work is difficult to categorize because it sits between disciplines. And so the burden of the first man's life and mind becomes the second man's burden. I think it's sort of based on Wittgenstein.

M I just know that Wittgenstein said that meaning comes from behavior, and Quine followed that too, if I'm not mistaken. It's amazing how I forget these things. I remember being in a class talking about something related to this and saying the right things.

F Hahaha, tell me about it.

M LOL. But now I can't remember accurately.

F Story of my life. I used to be smart and now I am borderline retarded.

M Haha.

F Sometimes I think it's a joke that I'm a professor because I can look like an idiot just groping for words up there in front of the students.

M LOL.

F But then at the end some write me letters to say mine was the best class they had.

M That must feel nice.

F Well, during the entire semester it feels like hell, I mean really fucking bad, I want to kill myself. I think they can tell. Haha. I am pathologically open.

M That's a good thing.

F I guess it works for me, but it's painful and exhausting.

M Why is it painful? No feedback?

F Hahahahaha. So I forgot. I wanted to say, about Robert Walser. There is this book of his, *The Robber*. I had no idea who this guy was, if he was important, interesting, anything. I really had no context for the book. Just started reading it and was so in love with him.

M You fall in love with a lot of writers. LOL.

F Yes, but I don't fall in love with everyone. I mean every writer, haha. And Robert Walser was like a crazy dirty tramp.

M He killed himself.

F So did David Foster Wallace.

M How old was he?

F Mid 40's.

M Young.

F Yes, and the director character in 8½ is also mid 40s, my age. And there's a scene where he has to hold a press conference and tell everyone what his film is about. And, while he's going up there to this giant empty rocket launching tower – the thing I told you about before, remember – the phallic symbol without the phallus that is supposed to be the centerpiece of the film? And he really doesn't want to go up there; he really can't face it.
And he gets to the table with the microphones and he just climbs under the table and says, "one minute, I'm thinking of what to say" and then shoots himself.

M Wow. That's very strong.

F But it turns out it's only a fantasy sequence. But oh my god that blew my mind.

M That reminds me. I saw once this director go on stage to speak about his movie. He answered the audience questions and it was funny because he acted kind of weird. He seemed autistic.

F Haha. Yes there's this great Picasso quote. I can never remember it exactly, it even rhymes. I used it in a poem once. It's about that gap between what an artist does and what he says about what he does.

M Picasso was brilliant.

F Haha yeah, I never really got into him until I read this book about the lifelong competition between him and Matisse. And it went into detail about their muses.

M I tend to maintain a bit of distance to all that has to do with art and culture. I think there are more important things.

F Is that a cautious distance?

M Maybe. Or maybe I just don't feel passionate about most things in general.

F Hahaha.

M Except for music. There's these works I love to know and know that I know them. It's not the same as recalling them.

F Do you read music?

M Well, I can read. I mean, I can't read only in my head, but with a piano, yes. I think I'm not able to play it now. I haven't played for ages. It would sound terrible.

F I'm sure it would sound good to me.

M Oh no. That's the thing about it. You must invest a lot of time and hard work. No good for lazy people like me. Hehe.

F You should see whether the novel called *The Loser* is translated. It's by Thomas Bernhard, same guy who wrote the book I was talking about earlier. It's told from the point of view of a guy who studies with Glenn Gould.

M I posted that on my Facebook some time ago.

F Wait. What? You posted that on Facebook?

M *The Loser,* yeah. I read that a long time ago.

F Wow, do I get extra points for that? I'm so good. And to think I picked you for some body parts.

M LOL.

F I'm really proud of myself over here, you should see me.

M LOL.

F I love love love Thomas Bernhard. He also killed himself.

M Why do they all kill themselves?

Postscript

My Best Thing is an extension of a short animation initially screened as part of *I've Had it and a Half*, a series of vignettes performed by Frances Stark in the Spring of 2011. The performance was the first time Stark presented transcripts from online sex-chat exchanges, which she had been collecting for over a year. Parts of dialogue were presented using simple lines of text projected in short legible fragments on an otherwise blank screen. The longest of the conversations was animated using Xtranormal, free 3D movie-making software. It was the impetus for *My Best Thing*, later becoming the second episode in the feature length animation. In the performance transcribed online chats were screened in segments, presented between other short sequences – a cameo by the artist showing random slides of her work and reading from personal emails, or a video of her last performance with everything edited out except her disfluencies – 'ums' and 'ahs.'

I've Had it and a Half was an accumulation of parts, pieces of conversations, fragments, quotes from essays and letters, and a random selection of images. The amassing of these components did form an aggregate, constituting a performance from beginning to end, but they didn't coalesce into a representative whole, building to a centralized point. Much of the performance's value rested in the definition of the varied parts, de-emphasizing a firm overall subject. *My Best Thing* is a reversal of this structure, having been transformed from a shorter version into a cohesive feature length narrative. This move from delimited parts to a comprehensive whole is a conscious one. As referenced in *My Best Thing* Stark knows the work will encounter a distracted audience, anticipating that most people will not see the piece in its entirety. Regardless, she commits to presenting a storyline that develops through linear sequences. It is a marked difference from Frances' earlier work, which privileged each divergent part as a strategy of openness. She hasn't abandoned this but instead uses a narrative structure to unify them. 'What will you say, finally, when you have seen the whole of all the parts as well as the parts of all the parts?' is a question first posited by the early twentieth century Polish writer Witold Gombrowicz, and a reoccurring quote used by Stark. It articulates the binary of whole and part, but doesn't prescribe an order; instead it infers that the two combined creates anticipation, insinuating that one shouldn't be offered without the other in mind.

Jenifer Papararo
Curator, Contemporary Art Gallery

Contributors

Mark Godfrey is Curator at Tate Modern in London. Prior to his appointment at the Tate in 2007, he was a lecturer in History and Theory of Art at the Slade School of Art, University of College London. He is the author of *Abstraction and the Holocaust* (Yale University Press, 2007) and *Alighiero E Boetti* (Yale University Press, 2011), as well as the survey essay in *Anri Sala* (Phaidon, 2005). He has published recent catalogue essays on Sharon Lockhart, Christopher Williams, Thomas Demand, Simon Starling, Tacita Dean, and others, and contributed an essay to the catalogue *Light Years: Conceptual Art and the Photograph* (Art Institute of Chicago, 2011). In 2007 Godfrey curated *Matthew Buckingham: Play the Story* at the Camden Arts Centre, London, and in 2009–2010, *Roni Horn aka Roni Horn*, a joint travelling exhibition organized between the Tate Modern and the Whitney Museum of American Art. He curated *Francis Alÿs: A Story of Deception* in 2010 and co-curated *Gerhard Richter: Panorama* in 2011 and *Alighiero Boetti: Game Plan* in 2012. He is currently working on retrospectives of Sigmar Polke and Richard Hamilton. He is also a frequent contributor to publications such as *Artforum*, *frieze*, and *October*.

Frances Stark is a Los Angeles based artist and writer whose practice is centered on language and the interrelation between graphic and textual materials in various forms of collage, performance, publishing and video. Her solo exhibition *The Fall of Frances Stark*, toured to Van Abbemuseum, Eindhoven; FRAC Bourgone, Dijon (2007); and Culturgest, Lisbon (2008). *A retrospective But What of 'Frances Stark,' Standing By Itself, a Naked Name, Bare as a Ghost To Whom One Would Like to Lend a Sheet* travelled to Nottingham Contemporary, Nottingham (2009); and Centre for Contemporary Arts, Glasgow (2010). Stark has been featured in group exhibitions including *Fit to Print*: Printed Media in Recent Collage, Gagosian Gallery, New York (2007); *Learn to Read*, Tate Modern, London (2007); *Poor. Old. Tired. Horse.*, ICA, London (2009); *Following A Line*, Contemporary Art Gallery, Vancouver; and *All of This and Nothing*, Hammer Museum in Los Angeles. Stark is also the author of *The Architect and the Housewife* (1999); *Collected Writings: 1993–2003* (2003), both published by Book Works, London. Since premiering at the 2011 Venice Biennale *My Best Thing* has screened at The Walter Phillips Gallery, The Banff Centre; The Institute of Contemporary Arts, London; The Marc Foxx Gallery, Los Angeles; and the Contemporary Art Gallery, Vancouver.

Colophon

This book is published on the occasion of *My Best Thing* at Walter Phillips Gallery, Banff (Sept. 24 – Dec. 11, 2011) and Contemporary Art Gallery, Vancouver (Feb. 3 – Apr. 8, 2012)

Text by Mark Godfrey
Edited by Jenifer Papararo
and Kitty Scott
Copy edited by William Wood
Designed by Selitsch Weig
Published by Koenig Books Ltd
Production by DZA Druckerei zu Altenburg GmbH

First published by Koenig Books, London
Co-published by: Contemporary Art Gallery ; Walter Phillips Gallery

ISBN 978-3-86335-142-7
(Koenig Books)

ISBN 978-1-897302-54-5
(Contemporary Art Gallery, Walter Phillips Gallery)

Printed in Germany

Bibliographic information published by the Deutsche Nationalbibliothek

The Deutsche Nationalbibliothek lists this publication in the Deutsche Nationalbibliografie; detailed bibliographic data are available in the Internet at http://dnb.d-nb.de

Library and Archives Canada Cataloguing in Publication

Godfrey, Mark Frances Stark :
my best thing / Mark Godfrey.

1 . Stark, Frances, 1967- --Criticism and interpretation. I. Stark, Frances, 1967- II. Contemporary Art Gallery (Vancouver, B.C.) III. Title.
N6537.S73G63 2012 709.2
C2011-907508-3

Distribution:

Buchhandlung Walther König, Köln
Ehrenstr. 4, 50672 Köln
Tel. +49 (0) 221 20 59 6 53
verlag@buchhandlung-walther-koenig.de

Contemporary Art Gallery
555 Nelson Street, Vancouver
British Columbia, Canada, V6R 6R5.
Tel. +1 604 681 2700
info@contemporaryartgallery.ca

Walter Phillips Gallery
The Banff Centre
107 Tunnel Mountain Drive,
Banff, Alberta T1L 1H5
Tel. +1 403 762 6281
walter_phillipsgallery@banffcentre.ca

UK & Eire
Cornerhouse Publications
70 Oxford Street
GB-Manchester M1 5NH
Tel. +44 (0) 161 200 15 03
publications@cornerhouse.org

US
D.A.P. / Distributed Art Publishers, Inc.,
155 6th Avenue, 2nd Floor
USA-New York, NY 10013
Tel. +1 (0) 212 627 1999
eleshowitz@dapinc.com

Images are stills from Frances Stark's *My Best Thing*, digital video, duration 99 minutes, 2011, and are courtesy the artist, Marc Foxx, Los Angeles; Gavin Brown's Enterprise, New York City; greengrassi, London and Daniel Buchholz, Cologne.

Acknowledgments

The Contemporary Art Gallery is generously supported by the Canada Council for the Arts, the City of Vancouver and the Province of BC through the BC Arts Council and the BC Gaming Policy and Enforcement Branch. We are also grateful for our members, donors, and volunteers.

The Walter Phillips Gallery is generously supported by the Canada Council for the Arts, the Alberta Foundation for the Arts and Canadian Heritage.

BRITISH COLUMBIA ARTS COUNCIL
An agency of the Province of British Columbia

Alberta Foundation for the Arts

CITY OF VANCOUVER

BRITISH COLUMBIA

Canada Council for the Arts / Conseil des Arts du Canada

Canadian Heritage / Patrimoine canadien

The Banff Centre

CAG

KoenigBooks